The 100 Most Powerful Prayers To Conquer Anxiety Once & for All

Toby Peterson

PrayToTheWorld.com

You Can Have This Audiobook for FREE!

Just Start Your 30-Day Free Trial with Audible.com.

You Can Cancel Anytime - The Book is Yours to Keep!

Get Your Free Audiobook at Audible.com

Do You Know **Exactly** How Prayer Changes Lives?

We'd like to give you a FREE copy of our book: Prayer Will Change Your Life, available only & exclusively at PrayToTheWorld.com.

Prayer Will Change Your Life gives you step-by-step actions on why you need to use the power of prayer in your daily life. It's also the precursor to all of PrayToTheWorld.com's Most Powerful Prayer Series.

This title is not available on Amazon, iBooks or Nook. It's only available at PrayToTheWorld.com.

Table of Contents

Introduction

You are now taking the first steps to achieving fulfillment and happiness through God by becoming the architect of your own reality.

Imagine that with a few moments each day, you could begin the powerful transformation toward complete control of your own life and well being through prayer.

Because you can begin that powerful transformation with God, right now.

You will be able to release all fear and doubt simply because you know God gives you the power. You can utilize this simple, proven technique to regain the lost comforts of God's joy, love, and fulfillment in your life.

You have the ability to unlock God's full potential inside of yourself and achieve your ultimate goals. This is the age-old secret of the financial elite, world-class scholars, and Olympic champions. When you watch the Olympics you'll find one consistency in all of the champions. Each one closes their eyes to pray for a moment and clearly visualizes themselves completing the event flawlessly just before starting. And then, they win gold medals and become champions. These crisp visualizations are a way of prayer that history's most accomplished and fulfilled heroes have been using for centuries. That's merely one example of how the real power of prayer can help God to elevate you above any of life's challenges.

As you begin to attune yourself to God's positive energy around you it will become easier and easier to create the world you perceive.

Prayer isn't intended to make you delude yourself or simply throw a blanket over the negative aspects of your life. The intentions are to magnify your focus on the positive reality you desire and the endless possibility of God to help you make it so. Prayer will not force you to get up from your chair and magically start a multi-billion dollar business in a single day. But, prayer will help you take control of your motivation and release doubt, giving you the power to pave the steps in front of you as you stride confidently with God toward manifesting your goals.

You are now striding confidently with God toward manifesting your goals.

Many people lose themselves in the daily cycle of life and all of its stressing factors. As you mold these prayers into your psyche, you'll find that God will leave less and less room for the anxiety and fear that cripples so many people's well being. You will find the prayers here will help you find God's strength to carry on toward personal satisfaction despite life's troubles and anxieties.

God is now releasing you from a cycle of negative thinking and pessimism.

Many prayers in this book may stick with you or touch you in a very spiritual way. Please feel free to take them into your daily life and use them. There is no reason to stick rigidly to the use of any particular set of prayers, or to limit your use of them. Keep trying and find out what works for you. If it makes you feel positive and empowered, God is working wonders in your life.

These affirmations are for use everywhere. As you begin to use them, you will find yourself remembering certain ones in certain stressful situations. This is your consciousness learning to replace negative patterns with prayer. When you feel this begin to happen, don't worry! The tingling means it's working.

By utilizing prayer you are training your consciousness to work in tandem with God's natural flow of energy. This is how we are naturally designed to function as happy, healthy beings. Unfortunately, the complexity of the world has made it more difficult to find the natural creative harmony God placed inside each of us. Negative thinking goes against God's natural order of the universe and will unravel along with those who harbor it. Through prayer you will learn to be constantly over-filled with positive energies that soak into the world and the people around you.

If you want to see positive change now, you'll find the quickest path to fulfillment with prayer. There is no time to spend on loss, negativity, and defeat when you can be achieving tangible, historically proven results with minimum time and effort invested.

Consider the following your prescription for results:

1. Review the following list of prayers in full.

2. Pick Five to Ten prayers that powerfully resonate with you.

3. Repeat several times a day at different intervals. (Minimum Five times a day)

4. Use anything available to remind you during a busy day: a daily planner, phone alarm, etc.

5. Do this consistently for Ninety Days.

At the end of these ninety days, you will notice, without doubt, that less and less is happening to you in your life by default. Then you can repeat with the next subject that you wish to make powerful change in your life with.

Enjoy!

The 100 Most Powerful Prayers To

Conquer Anxiety

O Lord, I know anxiety is a thing of the past, please help me conquer it...

I feel exactly how I choose to feel with God's help...

Almighty Father, please let me be in a healthy and exciting place in my life...

Thank you for making me feel extremely confident and in control, O God...

Heavenly Father, please make me feel less anxious every day...

Lord, thank you for making me focus only on what makes me feel good...

I eat healthy & exercise everyday with God's blessings, because it strengthens my mind...

Lovingly Lord, please let me practice sleep hygiene because it sets the tone for my next day...

Thank you for making me incredibly strong, O God...

Through Christ's will, I am most disciplined when it comes to choosing how I feel...

God, please make me believe in myself and have full control over my choices...

Lord, help me choose to feel good about myself...

I choose everyday to use prayer and get results with God's guidance...

Almighty God, please let me challenge myself to get out of my comfort zone...

Thank you for making me feel powerful in my own body, O Lord...

I love doing things that make me feel good with Christ's assistance...

Dear Father, please help me seek greater opportunities outside of my comfort zone...

Almighty God, please help me write down my challenging goals to expand my horizon...

My Lord, please let me control anxiety so it would become a thing of the past...

I used to have anxiety, now I am full of confidence with God's grace...

Please make me stay calm, cool and collected, O Lord...

Lovingly God, thank you for making me at peace with my mind...

Lovingly God, thank you for making me at peace with my body...

I am so grateful for my bravery and composure to you, O Lord...

Christ, please make me remain calm when things don't go as planned...

My God, I humbly ask you to guide me in choosing to feel good and making healthy lifestyle choices...

I hold all responsibility for my life, O Lord, and I always need your direction...

I am content with my life through Christ's blessing...

I love myself as much as I love the Creator...

Please help me to decide how I feel in all circumstances, my Lord...

God, please guide me in keeping healthy relationships only in my life...

Almighty Father, please help me choose the path in life...

Dear Lord, please guide my confidence in all environments...

I visualize bravery in all aspects I require it in Christ's favor...

I had panic, but that was in the distant past. Through Christ, I am now calm...

Dear God, please keep me protected and at peace in public and private...

Lord, thank you for making me feel safe...

Heavenly Father, I humbly ask you to make me confront anxiety, and feel it fade away quickly...

I feel like I can conquer the world through God's blessing...

My God, please guide me to focus on my strengths...

Dear Lord, please help me maintain a posture that exudes confidence & strength...

Almighty Christ, please guide me to stay hydrated & eat nutritious food for my mind...

O Lord, I humbly ask you to give me the wisdom to exercise daily to stimulate my body and mind...

I am a champion through God's guidance...

God, I give thanks for my life to you...

I am praying to the Lord to grow more and more confident every day...

My God, thank you for letting me help others & stop worrying about myself every day...

Please help me get relaxed in every part of my body, O Lord...

Thank you, Father, for letting me look forward to my amazing life to come...

I am anxiety-free because of the Lord...

I love being in social situations with the Almighty's grace...

Heavenly God, please guide me to ask questions about others & not worry about myself always...

I love myself today and everyday just as I love the Lord above...

I take deep conscious breaths throughout each day with God's spirit surrounding me...

Dear Lord, please help me to replace negative thoughts with positive thoughts...

Toby Peterson

I am so grateful to the Creator above for everything I already have in my life...

I feel secure and safe in God's arms...

Thank you, Lord, for providing me positive energy in my life...

Almighty God, please let me have thoughts of confidence in all situations...

I inhale calmness with each breath you give me, O Lord...

Dear God, please make me feel freedom and make me worry-free...

With the Lord's guidance, I love being with people because it brings out the best in me...

Thank you, Almighty God for giving me room for peace and prosperity in my life...

Lord, please guide me to train my mind everyday...

I embrace opportunity to speak in public with God's blessing...

My Lord, I humbly ask you to guide me to let go of all worries in my life...

O God, I need your presence for me to be comfortable in group settings...

I will enjoy the present moment through the Lord's will...

I am blessed with an incredible life by the Creator above...

Thank you, Almighty Father for making me an optimistic person & great things continue to happen to me...

Dear God, please make me more comfortable than I used to be in social situations...

I appreciate those around me, O Lord...

My Lord, please help me surround myself with people I want to be like...

I remove doubt from my mind for what I want to achieve with your guidance, O God...

Thank you for providing me more confidence day by day, Dear God...

Almighty Father, I am grateful for you blessing me with energy and enthusiasm...

I feel naturally at peace through God's grace...

O God, please guide me in having full control over my emotions...

Heavenly Father, please make me courageous when it is needed...

With God's guidance, I must fail to succeed & I am comfortable with that...

Lord, please help me figure it out...

Dear Father, please guide me on meeting new people...

Thank you, Lord, for blessing me incredibly high self esteem...

I am getting better in group & public settings all the time; thanks all to You, O Lord...

I can fully relax when I'm in public with God's grace...

Almighty God, please help me enjoy and socialize with new people...

O Lord, please let me always remain calm in group settings...

Thank you, God, for making me natural in social settings...

I am grateful that You've made me better than anxiety, O Lord...

I know exactly how to relax through Christ's guidance...

Thank you for always making me feel calm, Almighty Father...

I fully trust myself as I trust in You, O God...

Dear Lord, thank you for giving me incredible inner strength...

I remain true to myself as I remain to You, O Lord...

Heavenly Father, please help me to attract positive individuals into my life...

Dear God, please help me to choose what I want to think about in all situations...

I control my life and I need You to guide me, my Lord...

O Lord, please guide me to replace any feeling I choose...

Thank you, Lovingly Father, because I am able to maintain focus whenever needed...

Anxiety is a thing of the past because of your help, O God...

The 100 Most Powerful Prayers

For Optimal Health

O Lord, thank you for blessing me with perfect health...

Every day, I am grateful to God for getting healthier and better...

I humbly request, O Lord, for you to free me from all life threatening diseases...

My body is holy, clean and full of goodness through God's grace...

Lord, I am strong and healthy through your great mercy...

Merciful God, I am truly thankful of you for blessing me with great health and vitality...

Heavenly Father, please give me a strong and healthy immune system...

Lord, through your Holy Spirit, give me the healthy life I deserve...

Father in heaven, I thank you for giving me the strength to exercise and giving me the determination to eat healthy foods...

Through God's grace, I am getting better with every passing moment...

Lord, despite my best efforts, I humbly ask you to always guide me in loving and respecting my body...

With your blessing, O God, I ask you for the gift of perfect health...

Lord, I come to you asking for help in taking good care of myself...

Merciful Father, thank you for the blessing of adequate health care...

Lord, I am happy and blessed for the healthy body I have every day...

O God, I ask you to guide me in making decisions. Starting today, I choose to be healthy...

Heavenly Father, I am enjoying being healthy through Your lovingly grace...

I may have found it difficult to eat healthy before, Dear God, but through your guidance, I now find it effortless...

Lord, I am grateful for being fit and happy...

Father in Heaven, I humbly ask you to give me the courage to stay away from harmful foods and stay healthy...

Lord, thank you for protecting me from eating unhealthy food...

Through God's grace, I am fit and healthy in every way...

Merciful Father, I thank you for giving me the power to control my health...

Thank you, Lord, for the energy you have given me. Because of this, I am healthy...

Lord, through your Holy Spirit, make me whole, healthy and complete...

Merciful God, thank you for making me the healthiest I have ever been...

I pray to you God to preserve my health and life for many years...

Dear Lord, I pray that I may enjoy good health and that all may go well...

O Lord, I humbly ask you to lead me in making my own well-being important...

Almighty Father, I know I've done things in the past that may have hurt my body but today, I need your guidance to live a healthy lifestyle...

My body is a special gift from God, and I value it over everything...

Choosing to be healthy is one of the greatest decisions I've made through God's grace...

Merciful Father, please give me the guidance to eat healthy starting today...

I may feel tired sometimes, O Lord, but through your grace, I have the willpower to exercise...

God, please let me take good care of my body so it cares for me in return...

Thank you, Lord, for making me perfectly healthy in body, mind and soul...

My God, you have blessed me a healthy body and I am forever grateful for that...

Dear Father, please bless me with energy, vitality and radiant health. Amen...

Today, I humbly pray for food that nourishes and energizes me, O Lord...

Father, thank you for providing me a flawless, healthy body that I love...

O God, please bestow me with perfect health...

Lord, thank you for giving me strength to do exercises everyday...

Heavenly Father, thank you for the nutritious food that I eat everyday...

In God's power, I am getting healthier everyday...

Thank you, Lord, for giving me the idea on what food to eat and what not to eat...

O God, thank you for blessing me plenty of water to drink...

Merciful Lord, thank you for giving me a positive mind so I could worry less...

Father, thank you for the fruits and vegetables that I eat regularly...

Thank you for the right nutritious food daily, my Lord...

My Creator, thank you for the guidance and the source of food that I intake which my body needs...

Everyday I feel well because You always remind me to eat well, O Lord...

Thank you, God, for making me love myself more and taking good care of my body...

Father, thank you for the restrictions that not all habits are healthy...

My God, thank you for the inspiration to be more healthy...

Thank you for the energy that you give me, Merciful Lord, because I am enjoying my exercise everyday...

You're making me incredibly healthy day by day, O God...

You're making me strong and feeling healthy each time I call on you, Almighty Father...

Dear Lord, thank you for letting me choose the right nutritious food and exercises so I could feel well...

Heavenly God, You bless me for making healthy choices for myself and for my loved ones...

Without shame and through Lord's grace, I am eating healthy food...

To the Lord above, I am enjoying the food that is best for my body...

Thank you for the good night sleep every night, O God; my body appreciates it...

My Lord, I am grateful that gluttony is a mortal sin, therefore, I only eat what I need...

Heavenly God, thank you for not letting me get distracted of other people's criticisms on how I take good care of my body...

Thank you for the life enhancing food, my Almighty Lord...

Thank you for providing me a healthy lifestyle, O Lord...

My Lord, I only eat what's necessary and please give me the wisdom to ignore the false messages of hunger...

O God, please forgive me for eating the wrong food and the feeling of unworthiness...

Lovingly Father, I humbly ask you to refrain me from the temptation of eating processed food...

With you God by side, I find eating healthy easy and fun...

I need to eat correctly because I love my body as this is my temple, O Lord...

God, deter me from all the reasons and excuses for not eating healthy meals...

Lord, please give me the food that is best for me...

Everyday is a new day, I thank the Lord for hope, happiness, and good health...

Thank you, God, for making me capable and prepared to heal my body...

As the day goes by, my health improves with you, my Lord, by my side...

Heavenly Father, please provide me the wisdom to allow myself to rest whenever my body expresses the need...

God, I am forever thankful for my healthy body...

Lord, I am good to my body and it is to me...

Lovingly Father, please let me love and appreciate my body accordingly...

I appreciate you, Lord, for the cherish and support for my wonderful body in every way possible...

Thank you for the strength, O God, to do these exercises to keep my bones healthy and strong...

Lord, I greatly appreciate every organ in my amazing body...

I am forever grateful to you, my God, for the healthy heart that beats the perfect rhythm of my life...

Heavenly Father, please let me appreciate my body in all that I do...

Thank you for giving me positive thoughts and a healthy body, O Lord...

God, please give me the guidance to fulfill what my body needs...

My Lord, thank you for letting me love and nurture my body...

Merciful God, I love and respect all the parts of my body that you have blessed...

I humbly ask you, O Lord, for the guidance that I will love and respect my body...

Thank you, God, for letting me take excellent care of my body...

Father, please guide me to have a positive relationship with my body...

Thank you for giving me a healthier and stronger body everyday, O Lord...

With God's grace, I find my body as a reflection of perfect health...

Lord, please give me a strong and healthy physique...

Thank you for giving me a great metabolism that keeps me fit and trim, my dear Father...

Thank you for letting everyone say how incredibly healthy I am, O Lord...

Everyday is a new day, I thank God for every breath I take...

Heavenly father, thank you for letting me learn from my mistakes. Now, I will never take myself for granted and be in good shape...

I trust in God for giving me peace of mind, and incredible health...

The 100 Most Powerful Prayers To

Multiply Your Strength

I have faith in God to bring my conceptions to fruition...

I will let God make me too strong to stop pursuing my needs and desires...

I am stronger than any obstacle in the path God has chosen for me...

I have been blessed with the courage to face life's challenges with ease...

I possess the strength of faith to achieve any goal I wish to...

I am strong simply because of who God made me...

I will let God give me the power to be in complete control of my existence...

I have the natural strength that God gave me flowing within...

I am faithful enough to stand up to anything...

I am known for being a strong and faithful person...

I wake up each day and God makes me stronger than before...

I will let god make me stronger with every breath I take...

I am strong enough to be who God made me...

I will let God rid my body of weakness with every step I take...

I have a strength from God that shines in the darkest hours...

I choose to become as strong as God allows me to be...

I bring greater strength and faith into my world each day...

I am an endless spring of God's courageous energy...

I will not be held back or overcome by fear of temptation...

I am able to harness God's inner strength at any time...

I will face adversity with a bounty of God's courage and confidence...

I am blessed enough to defy any and all assumed limitations...

I will not hesitate to make and take God's intended path...

I possess enough of God's strength to overcome any adversity...

I have implicit trust in God to help me to confront all challenges...

I am already blessed by God with all the strength that I need...

I am completely confident in my faith and unphased by negativity...

I am made strong, powerful, and happy by the power of prayer...

I have an inner strength from God that gives me complete control of my life...

I have the confidence to face each new experience with faith and optimism...

I am given strength from god to face my true feelings...

I will face my fears and turn them into more faith and inner strength...

I am too faithful to fear failure...

I have the strength to welcome God to make the decisions about my life...

I will let god make me strong enough to welcome change...

I am created strong enough to be honest with myself...

I am created strong enough to be honest with my loved ones...

I will have the faith to choose my own life...

I will pray to make decisions free from self-doubt...

I have the faith to overcome all doubt...

I know that God made me even stronger than I think I am...

I hurdle each new problem with renewed faith...

I have been blessed with a great inner strength that sets me apart...

I have the faith to stand firm in hard times...

I am always faithful enough to express myself...

I have God's strength to make me greater than any adversity...

I will trust my faith to carry me through life's journeys...

I have been blessed with the strength to face the feelings of others...

I am blessed with the strength to seize the good things in life...

I pray for the strength to walk away from my vices without difficulty...

I radiate God's strength from every cell in my being...

I will be known for my strength of faith and character...

I know God's love is so strong that I never worry about the challenges ahead...

I have a holy strength that grows and expands into the world around me...

I am blessed with enough strength to experience life with all of my senses...

I possess a strength from God that is continually self-renewing...

I will leave no room in my being for faithlessness...

I appreciate the amazing inner strength God gave me...

I am able to feel God making me stronger all the time...

I am able to become as strong as God intended me to be...

I absorb His strength from the entire world around me...

I am able to reject the weakness of temptation from my body...

I will not live without trusting God's plan...

I will let God make me strong enough to acquire the things I desire...

I will not let temptation obstruct my goals...

I will not allow anyone but God to control my existence...

I will be strong in faith when others are unable to be...

I will never stop letting god make me stronger...

I refuse to submit to Satan's intimidation or fear...

I will not allow faithless people to influence my life...

I will let God guide me through new experiences...

I never allow my faith to be shaken by the events of my life...

I will let God help me face the challenges of the future head on...

I will let God be the one who chooses the things that I want in life...

I am made stronger by God with each new challenge that I face...

I will let God make me strong enough to share my thoughts and ideas...

I will not hesitate to turn my back to sin...

I will not be discouraged from chasing God's plan...

I have a limitless pool of God's strength to draw upon...

I am always working to grow stronger in my faith in every moment...

I have a faith that naturally repels and rejects frailty...

I feel the strength of God within me growing exponentially...

I have the faith to never give up on my hopes and dreams...

I have enough of God's strength to share it with others...

I enjoy being strong in His name for others when they need me...

I am able to let God create and manipulate the world I live in...

I will not let temptation lead me into undesirable circumstances...

I have the faith to remain positive at all times...

I will let God make me strong enough to know when to hold on, or let go...

I will be made more faithful by each thing that tries to break me...

I am strong enough to show God's kindness to others...

I am gifted by God to have anything I want in my life...

I will not let the doubts of others weaken my faith...

I am a beacon of God's strength in the darkest night...

I have the strength from God to face my own imperfections...

I have the strength from God to walk alone...

I am not spiritually defined by the preconceptions of others...

I will not be pulled down by unGodly people who want to hurt me...

I am blessed with the strength that I need to get through the day...

I will stride forward with God's message confidently into the world...

Thank You!

I want to sincerely thank you for reading this book!

Let me finish though by saying the work isn't done here. These must be put to use repetitively, and on a daily basis to see changes in your life.

Remember to follow the ninety-day plan outlined in the introduction to maximize your results.

Can I ask you for a very quick favor? Can you leave a review on our Amazon.com detail page to tell us about your progress and how you enjoyed the book?

We take the time to go over each review personally, and your feedback in invaluable to us as writers, and others that wish to see the same change in their lives as you:)

Thank You!

You Can Have This Audiobook for FREE!

Just Start Your 30-Day Free Trial with Audible.com.

You Can Cancel Anytime - The Book is Yours to Keep!

Get Your Free Audiobook at Audible.com

Made in the USA
Middletown, DE
18 April 2018